CLARK

LET'S EXPERIMENT!

LET'S

EXPERIMENT!

CHEMISTRY FOR BOYS AND GIRLS

by JACQUELINE HARRIS STRAUS

Pictures by LEONARD KESSLER

HARPER & ROW, PUBLISHERS, NEW YORK AND EVANSTON

TO MY RESEARCH ASSISTANTS,

CAROL AND JOHN

CONTENTS

vi

A NOTE TO PARENTS

The experiments in this book have all been tried out by children between the ages of five and ten years. They have had a wonderful time with them. For a while chemistry was a neighborhood fad among this age group. They played with their sets for hours at a time, swapping chemicals and ideas as if they were trading cards.

The composition of the chemistry set itself seems to be almost as important to children of this age as doing the experiments. They want their set to look like the sets they can buy. This is one reason for the amount of space that has been devoted in this book to the description of the chemistry set that they should make. In this description I have told them what to use for test tubes. It is very important that they have this particular type and size of pill bottle. It is much easier to clean than a test tube. It is small—therefore their chemicals will last longer and if spilled there will be very little mess to clean up. This bottle is not as breakable or as easily tipped over as a test tube.

Chemistry is often regarded as too messy or too dangerous a hobby for young children, but my experience has not borne this out. It has not taken any longer to clean up after a session with chemistry experiments than it takes to clean up after the children have played with clay. And they are not nearly so messy as finger paints, for example.

The experiments in this book are not dangerous. With the exception of Experiment 13, none of the experiments requires the use of anything hotter than hot tap water. The "explosion" in Experiment 1 does not generate heat and is not dangerous. While a few of the experiments require the use of a weak solution of iodine and some ammonia, there has been no difficulty with these. The iodine in the form it is used is very much diluted. The children were quite impressed with the fact that iodine and ammonia are poisonous. Several of them insisted on washing their hands immediately if some spilled.

Every effort has been made to make this book readable by children at about the third grade level. The experiments, however, can be easily performed and understood by children considerably younger than this.

CHEMISTRY AND YOU

Long ago, people thought that everything in the world was made from fire or water or air or earth. Now we know that this is not so. Chemists have discovered that there are about one hundred ELEMENTS. Everything else is made by combining these elements, or substances.

Some chemists spend their time finding out why the elements behave as they do because they think this is interesting and important. Other chemists spend their time learning how to combine the elements into new things which people can use. You use the products of chemistry every day.

1

Here are just a few of the materials that chemistry has made possible:

Ink in any color

Glue that is stronger than the pieces stuck together

Nylon for clothes

Foam rubber for pillows

Plastics for toys

Soap that works in hard water

Paint that dries right away

Chemistry is a science. This means that it is not just a lot of facts. A science is a way of thinking. It is a way of finding out answers to problems. Chemists are one kind of scientist. Like all scientists, they want to find out as much as they can about the world. Scientists have many ways of finding out about the world:

They read what other scientists have written.

They try out experiments which other scientists have performed to see if they will work for them too.

They use their imagination to guess about the world. Then they experiment to see if their guesses were right.

They keep careful notes so that other scientists can also do the experiments they have done.

They invent new tools to help them see and measure the changes that take place.

If you like to see what happens when you mix and stir things together, you will have fun doing the experiments in this book. As you get older, you may want to learn more about what chemists have discovered. You may even want to figure out new ideas and then experiment to see if your ideas are right. Chemistry can be your hobby or you can make it your career. But even if you only do the experiments in this book, you will have a better understanding of the wonderful world in which you live.

MAKING YOUR CHEMISTRY SET

Here is a list of the things you will need to make your chemistry set:

SMALL BOTTLE WITH MEDICINE-DROPPER TOP

SPOONS (teaspoon and tablespoon)

TEST TUBES: Do not get regular test tubes. They break very easily, and they fall over unless you keep them in a special stand. Instead, buy pill bottles with plastic caps. Be sure these bottles are made of clear glass or plastic and that they have snap-on or plug caps, not screw-on tops. These pill bottles come in several sizes. The 5- or 6-dram size is just right for most of the experiments in this book. Get ten in this size and one or two in a larger size as well. The smaller size usually costs five cents, the larger size is usually ten cents.

TEN SMALL BOTTLES: You will keep your chemicals in these. It is best to have bottles all the same size. The set will be much neater looking and your bottles will take up less

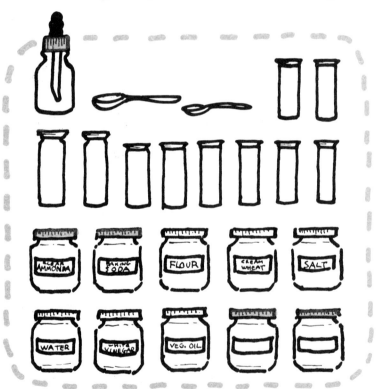

6

space. You can use any small bottles you can find around the house. The kind that baby food comes in is just right. You can also buy bottles at the drugstore. They cost about ten cents each. Ask for 4-ounce jars with screw-on tops.

ADHESIVE TAPE to label the bottles

Now you are ready to fill your bottles. Here is a list of the chemicals to put in them. You will need these for more than one experiment, so fill your bottles with them now. Label the bottles right away so you do not get them mixed up.

Clear ammonia

Baking soda

Flour

Cream of Wheat

Salt

Water

White vinegar

Vegetable oil

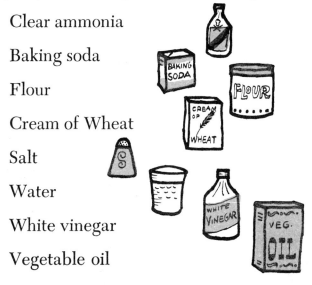

Some of the experiments call for things that are not on this list, but you will need only a little of these other chemicals. It is not necessary to get a whole jarful. Just wrap a spoonful of these other chemicals in a piece of waxed paper or put some in one of your small experiment bottles.

It is always best to take just a little of what you need. If you take the whole box of baking soda or the whole jar of vinegar, you might spill them or get the box wet or dirty. You can always go back for more when you need it.

To finish making your chemistry set, you will need a few more things:

A small bottle of tincture of iodine

Paper napkins

A drinking glass

A medium-sized tray

A box or basket to keep your set in

You can get along without everything on this last list except the iodine, so don't get upset if you can't find all of them.

8

USING YOUR SET

Chemistry is a laboratory science. A laboratory should be kept as neat as possible. Sometimes, however, things may spill or splash. Follow these few rules and no one will complain about your experiments being too messy.

1. Don't wear your best clothes.

2. Work in a room that you can clean up easily, such as the bathroom or basement.

3. Do your experiments on a tray to make it easier to clean up when you are through.

4. Don't leave any mess for your mother to clean up.

5. DON'T TAKE ANYTHING FROM THE KITCHEN OR BATHROOM UNLESS YOU ASK YOUR MOTHER IF YOU MAY HAVE IT. ASK HER EACH TIME.

You will have fun doing these experiments. Follow the directions at first. Smell your mixtures and feel them. Be alert to the changes that are taking place and try to understand what is happening. Then try out some of your own ideas. That is what experiment really means.

EXPERIMENT 1 BAKING-SODA EXPLOSION

You will need:

A TEST TUBE AND SEVERAL CAPS   TEASPOON

VINEGAR   BAKING SODA

What to do:

Fill the test tube about half full with vinegar.
Add one-quarter of a teaspoonful of baking soda.

The mixture will foam over the top right away. While it is still foaming, put a cap on it. The cap will pop off. You can replace the cap and have it pop off several times if you are quick. Sometimes it helps to shake the bottle a little.

What happens:

When baking soda and vinegar are mixed, they make a gas called carbon dioxide. When you blow up a balloon, you are filling the balloon with some of this same gas. If you keep on blowing long enough, the balloon breaks. The rubber in the balloon isn't strong enough to hold the gas in. The same thing has happened in this experiment. There isn't enough room in the bottle for all the gas that the baking soda and vinegar make. The gas pushed the lid up into the air.

Baking soda and an acid make carbon dioxide whenever they are mixed together. Vinegar is an acid. Fruit juices are acids also. You will be learning more about acids in other experiments.

You can tell from the name that baking soda is used in baking. When your mother makes a cake with sour milk, she uses baking soda. It fills the cake with little pockets of carbon dioxide. Without baking soda the cake would not rise and it would be mealy, sort of like a baked potato.

EXPERIMENT 2   ORANGE SODA

You will need:

A DRINKING GLASS	TEASPOON
WATER	BAKING SODA
ORANGE JUICE	SUGAR

What to do:

Fill the glass half full with water. Fill the glass the rest of the way with orange juice. Add half a teaspoon of baking soda. Stir it. Now you have a glass of soda. You may drink it.

You can make any kind of soda you like by using other kinds of fruit juices. Use different amounts of juices to suit your taste; sometimes as little as a tablespoon will do. Add sugar if you like.

What happens:

Another name for soda water is carbonated water. The fizzing you see in the glass is bubbles of carbon dioxide gas. The bubbles were formed when you combined the baking soda with the juice. In Experiment 1 you got a lot of foam because there was so much carbon dioxide formed all at once. The foam was all these bubbles bunched together in a tiny bottle. In this experiment they have more room to spread out.

EXPERIMENT 3   DANCING MOTHBALLS

You will need:

A GLASS OF WATER   FOUR OR FIVE MOTHBALLS

TEASPOON   VINEGAR

BAKING SODA

What to do:

Add one-half teaspoon of baking soda to the

glass of water. Stir it until it is dissolved. Drop the mothballs into the glass. Add vinegar very slowly until the mothballs rise to the top.

If the mothballs sink and do not come up, you should slowly add a little more vinegar. When they sink and rise over and over again, you have added just the right amount of vinegar. The mothballs will "dance" for about an hour. When they stop, you can start them again by adding more vinegar.

What happens:

If you have done Experiments 1 and 2, you will know that the tiny bubbles you see are carbon dioxide gas. They are lighter than the water. The bubbles get stuck to the rough sides of the mothballs and lift them to the top of the glass. When the mothballs get to the top of the glass, some of the carbon dioxide bubbles break loose. The mothballs are heavier than the water, so if they do not have the bubbles to hold them up, they sink. On the bottom of the glass they collect more carbon dioxide bubbles and are lifted to the top again.

EXPERIMENT 4   TESTING FOR ACID WITH RED CABBAGE

You will need:

RAW RED CABBAGE

ONE-QUART JAR

HOT WATER

TWO SMALL JARS

BAKING SODA

VINEGAR

TEST TUBES

TEASPOON

UNGLAZED WHITE PAPER OR
  NEWSPAPER

A BAKING PAN

PAPER NAPKINS

Some other things to test:

SHAMPOO

LAUNDRY SOAP

LEMON JUICE

ORANGE JUICE

DIRT

Some things to buy if you want to:

LITMUS PAPER   NITRAZINE PAPER

What to do:

Cut or tear the leaves of the cabbage and stuff the quart jar full of them. Pour hot water over them. Put the jar aside until the water in the jar looks purple. Pour a little out to see. When the water is purple fill one of your small jars with it. Label it "Cabbage Water." Save the rest of the water; you will need it a little later.

Now you are ready to test the baking soda and vinegar. Fill a test tube half full of water. Add a half-teaspoon of baking soda. Fill the test tube the rest of the way with cabbage water. The cabbage water will turn green.

Fill another test tube half full of vinegar. Now add some cabbage water. This time the cabbage water will turn pink.

Try your cabbage water on other things. Sometimes it will turn pink and sometimes it will turn green. Make a list of all the things that turn green and a list of all the things that turn pink. Anything which makes the cabbage water turn pink is an acid. Anything which makes it turn green is called a "base."

Now try the second part of this experiment. Cut the paper into strips about this size:

If you are using newspaper, use just the margins, where there is no printing. Lay the strips of paper in the baking pan. Pour the cabbage water that you have saved in the quart jar over them. Let the strips of paper soak until they have turned purple. Then take them out and set them to dry on the paper napkins.

These pieces of paper can be used instead of the cabbage water to find out whether something is an acid or a base. The paper will turn pink when dipped into an acid and it will turn green when dipped into a base.

You have to be careful with your paper because it can be spoiled by very small amounts of acids and bases. Be sure to wash and dry your hands carefully before you handle it. Keep it in one of your small jars.

What happens:

One way chemists have of describing a chemical is by the way it acts when it is mixed with other chemicals. Chemicals which make cabbage water turn pink are called acids. Acids also have a sour taste. Chemicals which make cabbage water turn green are called bases. Bases taste bitter and feel soapy or slippery. Acids and bases are opposites. When an acid and a base are mixed together, a new kind of chemical is formed. It is called a salt.

Many acids and bases are safe to handle, but others can be dangerous. Some acids and bases are so strong that they can eat holes in cloth and burn your skin. Even chemists do not touch the strong-est ones with their fingers.

Vinegar, lemon juice, grapefruit, and other foods that taste sour are acids. Most soaps are bases. Lime which is used for gardening is a base. When people add it to their soil, they say they are making the soil sweeter. A soil that is acid is called sour. Test some soil to see if it is an acid or a base. Is your saliva an acid or a base? Hold a piece of testing paper in your mouth to see.

Paper such as the kind you made can be bought in a drugstore. It is called litmus paper and comes in two colors, pink for testing bases and blue for testing acids. This paper won't do any better job for you than the paper you made.

Chemists have a way of describing how strong an acid or a base is. They say that an acid has a low pH and that a base has a high pH. Another kind of paper will tell you which acids and bases are stronger. This is called pH paper. Nitrazine paper is one brand of pH paper, and you can buy it in a drugstore. It is tan in color but will change to seven different shades when you use it. This paper is fun to use but it is expensive. A piece the size of the papers you made costs a penny.

EXPERIMENT 5

TESTING FOR STARCH WITH IODINE

You will need:

BOTTLE WITH MEDICINE-
DROPPER TOP

TEST TUBE

TINCTURE OF IODINE

TEASPOON

WATER

FLOUR

Please be careful:

There are two things you should know about iodine. It is poisonous. Do not leave it around where your little brothers or sisters can get at it. And it can make stains that will not wash out with water. Be very careful not to spill it.

Some other things to test:

CREAM OF WHEAT   SLICE OF POTATO

PAPER NAPKIN   SLICE OF BREAD

OTHER KINDS OF PAPER   SALT

MILK

What to do:

Before you begin this experiment you have to prepare your iodine solution. (*Be sure to get permission from your mother to take the iodine.*) Fill your medicine-dropper bottle about one-quarter full of iodine. Do this over the bathroom sink. Put the rest of the iodine away in the medicine chest where it belongs. Next fill the bottle the rest of the way to the top with water. Now you are ready to test for starch.

Fill a test tube half full with water. Add a quarter of a teaspoonful of flour and several drops of the iodine solution. Shake the test tube well each time. The liquid in your test tube will turn dark purple or black.

What happens:

Flour has starch in it. The starch and the iodine have formed a new chemical. This new chemical is dark purple or black. Whenever iodine is mixed with a substance which has starch in it, the starch and the iodine will form this new dark purple or black iodine-starch chemical.

Try this experiment on any other foods your mother can let you have. Try it on several kinds of paper. Make a list of all the foods and other things that you test for starch. Put a mark next to the ones that do have starch in them.

You eat a lot of starchy foods every day. They fill you up and give you the energy you need for playing. Starch has other uses too. Cornstarch or flour is used for making soup and gravy thick. Laundry starch helps to keep shirts and dresses neat looking. Another kind of starch is added to some papers to make them stiffer and heavier.

EXPERIMENT 6   INVISIBLE INK

You will need:

PAPER

IODINE SOLUTION USED
   IN EXPERIMENT 5

TEST TUBE

WATER

TABLESPOON

FLOUR

SMALL CLEAN PAINT-
BRUSH OR A PIECE OF
COTTON WRAPPED ON
THE END OF A TOOTH-
PICK

2 SMALL BOWLS

ORANGE OR LEMON
   JUICE

What to do:

Before you can do this experiment you will have

to test a piece of paper for starch. You must find a piece of paper that does not turn dark purple or black when you put a few drops of the iodine solution on it. This should not be too hard to do. Look for a piece of paper that is not glossy. Tablet paper should work.

Now fill the test tube half full with water. Add a teaspoonful of flour and shake it up well. Dip your brush into this "ink" and write with it. When the writing is dry, it will be invisible.

To make the writing appear, fill one of the small bowls with water and add several drops of your iodine solution to it. Then soak the piece of paper in the bowl of iodine solution. The writing will turn black.

You can also make the writing invisible again. Fill the second bowl with water. Add several tablespoons of orange or lemon juice. Soak the paper

in this bowl and the writing will disappear. If the writing does not appear or disappear, you need more iodine or juice in the bowls of water.

What happens:

In this experiment you are making two new chemicals. First you made the iodine-starch chemical—the same one as in Experiment 5. That makes the writing appear.

The writing disappears when you soak the paper in the orange or lemon juice because these juices are rich in Vitamin C. The Vitamin C combines with the iodine in the iodine-starch chemical to make the second new chemical, which is colorless. But the starch is still on the paper, and if you put the paper back into the iodine, you make the dark purple or black iodine-starch chemical again.

Lemon or orange juice can be used to remove iodine stains from clothing. The iodine is still there, but you cannot see it. The Vitamin C in the juice turns the iodine into a colorless liquid.

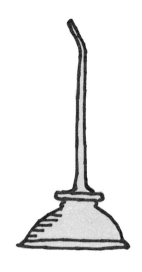

EXPERIMENT 7 TESTING FOR OIL

You will need:

TEST TUBES

WATER

VEGETABLE OIL

HAND LOTION

FURNITURE POLISH (NOT
FURNITURE CLEANER)

What to do:

Fill a test tube about half full with water. Add a

little of the vegetable oil to it. The oil will float on the top. Even if you shake the test tube very well, the vegetable oil will soon be floating on the top again. Now test the hand lotion and the furniture polish in the same way.

What happens:

Some chemicals will mix with others and some will not. Salt will dissolve in water but not in oil. Oil will not mix with water, but it will mix with alcohol. Chemists say that alcohol and oil have an attraction for each other and that oil and water do not have an attraction for each other.

If you weigh a bottle of oil and the same size bottle of water, you will discover that the bottle of oil weighs less than the bottle of water. Since the oil is lighter than the water and the two chemicals are not attracted to each other, the oil floats on top of the water, where you can easily see it when you do this experiment.

When two chemicals are attracted to each other, you can mix them together by stirring or shaking them. Chemists have also discovered ways of getting chemicals which are not attracted to each other to mix together and stay mixed.

If you test milk to see whether it has fat or oil in it, you probably will not see any oil floating on top of the water in your test tube. Yet milk has a lot of fat in it, and this all used to collect at the top of the bottle. People got tired of always having to shake up the milk before they used it, so dairy chemists discovered a way to mix it so that it would stay mixed. This kind of milk is called HOMOGENIZED milk. It is so well-mixed that the fat will not float when you mix the milk with water.

Peanut butter has fat in it too. It used to be that when you opened a jar of peanut butter there was a lot of oil floating on the top. Before you could use the peanut butter, you had to mix it up. This was hard to do. The people who make peanut butter asked chemists to solve this problem. These chemists found that by putting HYDROGEN into the peanut butter oil in a special way, the fat would stay mixed. This kind of peanut butter, with hydrogen in it, is called HYDROGENATED peanut butter.

If you look carefully at a carton or bottle of milk, you will find the word HOMOGENIZED. If you look carefully at a jar of peanut butter, you may find the word HYDROGENATED. Many other foods are homogenized and hydrogenated. Your test for oil will not work on these foods, but you will probably find one of these words on their containers.

EXPERIMENT 8
A SANDWICH IN A BOTTLE

You will have more fun with this experiment if you try Experiments 5 and 7 first.

You will need:

TEST TUBE

WATER

FLOUR

CREAM OF WHEAT

TEASPOON IODINE SOLUTION
MADE FOR EXPERIMENT 5

VEGETABLE OIL

33

What to do:

Fill the test tube about half full with water. Add the flour and Cream of Wheat—about one-quarter teaspoon of each. Then add a few drops of the iodine solution and a little oil. Shake the test tube well each time you add something. Let the bottle rest for a few minutes. When you look at it later, you will see several layers of chemicals.

Try making other kinds of "sandwiches." You can make some very pretty ones of your own.

What happens:

In other experiments in this book you learned that some chemicals dissolve in water and that others do not. The Cream of Wheat hardly dissolved at all. Most of it settled on the bottom of the test tube because it is the heaviest of the ma-

34

terials you added. The oil floats on the top because it is the lightest. Some of the flour dissolved in the water, but a lot of it settled to the bottom too. You know from Experiment 5 that starch and iodine make a black chemical. This explains the muddy color of the water and the darker-colored layer you see just above the Cream of Wheat.

EXPERIMENT 9 TESTING FOR COPPER

You will need:

A PENNY   CLEAR AMMONIA

A TEST TUBE

Please be careful:

Ammonia is a poison and it smells awful. You probably won't like the smell of it, but it won't hurt you if you are careful. A good strong sniff of it may make your nose bleed, so don't hold your face right over it when you are doing this experiment.

Other things to test:

A SMALL PIECE OF WIRE FROM AN OLD ELECTRIC CORD (ASK YOUR MOTHER OR FATHER TO HELP YOU FIND THIS)

OTHER COINS

OTHER PIECES OF METAL

What to do:

Put the penny in the bottom of the test tube.

Pour a little of the ammonia over it. Use just enough ammonia to cover the penny. The ammonia will turn blue. This shows that the penny has copper in it. The longer you leave the penny in the ammonia, the darker the blue will get.

Try this experiment on other coins and other pieces of metal. If they have copper in them, the ammonia will turn blue. With some of them you may have to wait longer for the ammonia to turn blue than you did with the penny. You will get faster results with old coins and pieces of copper than with shiny new ones.

What happens:

When you put the penny in the ammonia, a little of the copper combined with the ammonia and made a new chemical. This new chemical is a combination of the copper and the ammonia. It has its own special color—a deep blue. It is a different color from the ammonia and the copper that you started with because it is a different chemical.

One way you can tell if something is made of copper is by its color. A penny is almost all copper and it is copper colored. Dimes and nickels have some copper in them too. They are silver colored because of the other metals in them. So you can't always tell by the color if something has copper in it.

Copper is a very useful metal. Many people cook with copper-bottomed pots because copper carries heat well. Copper also carries electricity very well. This is why it is used for electric wires.

EXPERIMENT 10   MAKING CRYSTALS

You will need:

A SMALL JAR

HOT WATER

TABLE SALT

TABLESPOON

A PIECE OF STRING

A PIECE OF CARDBOARD

A PAPER CLIP, WASHER,
   OR NAIL

Other things you can use:

ALUM   WASHING SODA

BORIC ACID   EPSOM SALTS

What to do:

Fill the small jar with hot water. The water should be very hot, but tap water is hot enough. Add salt, a tablespoon at a time, stirring after you add each tablespoon. When the salt sinks to the bottom of the glass instead of dissolving, you have added the right amount.

Take the string, the cardboard, and the washer (or other weight) and arrange them as shown in the picture. The string should be just long enough to reach the bottom of the jar. Place the jar in a quiet warm place. To get large crystals it is very important to let the water cool slowly. The more slowly the crystals are formed, the larger they will be. After a few days you will have a string of large salt crystals which you can lift out of the jar.

You can make a collection of different kinds of crystals by dissolving alum, boric acid, washing soda, or epsom salts in hot water in the same way

40

as you did the salt. You can get these chemicals at a drugstore. Let these crystals grow on a string the same way you grew the salt crystals.

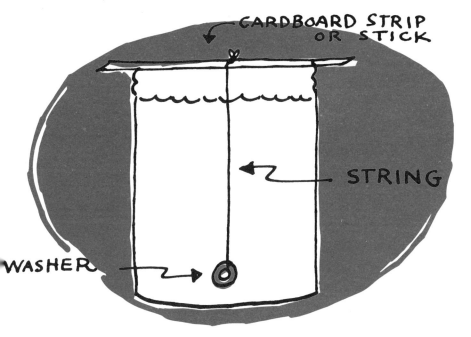

What happens:

When you dissolve salt in water, you have made a SOLUTION. The salt that you dissolve in the water is a crystal to begin with. In this experiment you added as much salt as you could make dissolve. As long as the water was hot, the salt stayed in solution. But when the water cooled, it could not hold the same amount of salt, so part of the salt changed back to its crystal form. More crystals formed later because part of the water evaporated. Your salt crystals were larger than they had been because you grew them slowly.

If you made more than one kind of crystal, you will see that each chemical has its own crystal shape.

Besides the crystals which you can make, you can find crystals all around you to add to your collection. Rock candy is just big crystals of sugar. Grains of sugar are smaller crystals. Grains of sand are crystals of quartz with their corners and edges worn off by the water and the wind. Rubies, sapphires, emeralds, and diamonds are all crystals but are too expensive to add to your collection!

EXPERIMENT 11

MAKING CURDS AND WHEY

You will need:

A TEST TUBE   VINEGAR

MILK

What to do:

Fill a test tube three-quarters full of milk. Fill it the rest of the way with the vinegar. Almost at once you will see the milk change. Down in the bottom of the test tube there will be a thick substance and on top will be a watery liquid. You can pour off this watery liquid and save the solid material on the bottom. The watery part is called whey. The solid part is the curds.

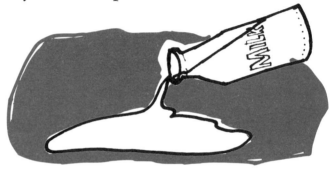

What happens:

Chemists have spent a lot of time studying milk. They have found that it is a combination of water, fat, proteins, carbohydrates, and minerals, and that it is rich in vitamins. When you added the vinegar, it made the milk turn sour and separated some of its parts.

44

The curds are the fat and minerals and one kind of protein called casein. All kinds of cheeses are made from the curds. Casein is used to make plastic toys. It is also used in making the white glue which you buy in squeeze bottles. In fact, you can use the curds you made in this experiment as glue. They will do a good job of sticking pieces of paper together. Try it and see.

EXPERIMENT 12   RUBBER BONES

You will need:

A WISHBONE   SMALL JAR OR DISH

VINEGAR

What to do:

It is important that the bone not be broken or cracked at the joint even a little bit if you want this experiment to work well.

Put the bone in the jar or dish. Cover it with vinegar and let it soak overnight. In the morning the bone will be very rubbery. It won't break.

What happens:

Bones have a lot of calcium in them. This same calcium is also found in limestones and is used to make cement. So you can see that anything that has a lot of calcium in it should be hard.

However, the calcium is easily dissolved by the acid in the vinegar. Without the calcium the bone becomes soft and rubbery. If you were to let the vinegar evaporate, you might be able to see the little hard grains of calcium in the bottom of the bowl.

You have probably eaten pickles. Pickles are cucumbers that have been soaked in vinegar. The acid in the vinegar keeps the pickle from spoiling and gives it a good flavor. The process of soaking something in an acid is called pickling. You could call this a pickled bone.

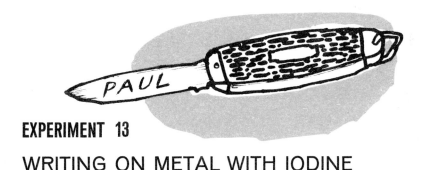

EXPERIMENT 13

WRITING ON METAL WITH IODINE

You will need:

YOUR POCKETKNIFE   A LARGE TEST TUBE

A PIECE OF FINE SANDPA-
PER OR STEEL WOOL

A CANDLE OR A PIECE OF
PARAFFIN

A NAIL

TINCTURE OF IODINE (*not*
the solution of iodine
and water that you
used in Experiments
5, 6, and 8)

Note: Do not use one of your mother's knives for this experiment. Most of her knives are made of stainless steel and it will not work on them anyway. Your pocketknife is probably not made of stainless steel. If it is, you can try this experiment on other pieces of scrap metal. It will work on some kinds of metal and not on others.

You will need quite a bit of iodine for this experiment. When you are through with it, do not leave the test tube of iodine lying around where your small brother or sister can get at it or where it might be spilled. Throw the iodine away right away, or ask your mother to put it in a safe place for you. Then you can use it to do this experiment again or to make more of the iodine solution you need for Experiments 5, 6, and 8.

What to do:

Clean the blade of your knife or the piece of metal with the sandpaper or steel wool. Next, warm the blade of the knife by holding it over a flame. (If you are using a piece of metal for the experiment, hold it with a pair of pliers or some similar tool so that you do not burn your fingers.) Now coat the blade with wax by rubbing it with the candle or paraffin. Let it cool.

When the blade is cool, write your initials in the wax with the nail. Be sure you write deeply enough to cut through the wax to the metal. Make your letters big and fat.

Fill the test tube with enough iodine to cover the writing on the blade. Soak the blade in the iodine, taking care that the knife does not tip over the test tube. After thirty minutes, take the blade out of the test tube and wash off the iodine with cold water. Heat the blade again and wipe off the wax. When all the wax is cleaned off you will see your initials written on the blade.

What happens:

Iodine leaves a mark on certain metals that won't come off. This mark is a kind of rust. The iodine can rust only the part of the metal that is not protected by the wax.

Putting a design or writing on metal in this way is called etching. Most etching is done with a strong acid that eats into the metal and makes a groove. The wax protects the rest of the metal from the acid. Often a metal plate with an etched design is used for printing. Many famous artists have etched beautiful pictures in this way. You might say these artists were chemists as well as artists.

MORE FUN WITH TESTS

Do you remember the excitement on your birthday when you tried to guess what was inside a mysteriously wrapped present? Its size and shape may have given you a clue. Before you opened the package you may have shaken it to see if it rattled. The feel of it—whether it was soft or hard—gave you another clue as to what the present might be. You may not have realized it, but you were testing it.

Some chemists spend a lot of time testing things to find out what they are made of. Some of their tests are quite simple. They notice the color and shape of the things they are testing. They smell and feel them to get clues to what they could be. And they perform tests like the ones in this book and many others besides. This kind of chemistry is called QUALITATIVE ANALYSIS. Qualitative analysis is in many ways like figuring out what is inside a surprise package, and it can be as exciting.

After you have done the experiments in this book, give a friend some of your chemicals and ask him to combine some of them. You will have to be careful what you give him. You can give him your ammonia, vegetable oil, baking soda, cabbage water, and one of the chemicals that has starch in it. You will need the iodine and vinegar for testing, so don't give him these.

Divide the mixture that he gives you into several test tubes. That way you can test for one thing at a time. You will probably be able to tell something about his mixture just by looking at it. A careful sniff will tell you if he has used the ammonia. The vinegar will make the baking soda fizz and the cabbage water turn pink. Use the iodine to test for the starchy chemical you gave him.

A MAGIC SHOW

Have you ever seen a magic show? Did you wonder how the magician could do such wonderful tricks? When you have done some of the experiments in this book, you can have a magic show of your own.

You can make purple cabbage water turn pink or green just by adding a vinegar or a baking soda solution to it.

You can make mothballs dance up and down in a glass.

Just by dropping a penny into a glass of a clear

colorless liquid (ammonia) you can make the liquid turn blue.

You can fool people with rubber wishbones and make writing appear on blank sheets of paper.

Be sure to say a few magic words when you are performing—the way real magicians do. People who do not know about these chemical reactions will be as fooled as you were by the magicians you have seen.